Resetting Economies *from the* COURTS OF HEAVEN

Resetting
Economies
from COURTS
the
OF HEAVEN

**5 SECRETS TO OVERCOMING
ECONOMIC CRISIS AND UNLOCKING
SUPERNATURAL PROVISION**

ROBERT
HENDERSON

DESTINY IMAGE® PUBLISHERS, INC.

P.O. Box 310, Shippensburg, PA 17257-0310

"Promoting Inspired Lives."

This book and all other Destiny Image and Destiny Image Fiction books are available at Christian bookstores and distributors worldwide.

Cover design by: Eileen Rockwell

For more information on foreign distributors, call 717-532-3040.

Reach us on the Internet: www.destinyimage.com.

ISBN 13 TP: 978-0-7684-5703-2

ISBN 13 eBook: 978-0-7684-5704-9

For Worldwide Distribution, Printed in the U.S.A.

1 2 3 4 5 6 7 8 / 24 23 22 21 20

CONTENTS

CHAPTER 1

CRISIS – DANGEROUS OPPORTUNITY

Crisis comes along periodically in life. Few worldwide crises occur however. Those which touch everyone and no one is exempt are quite infrequent. We however have faced just such a thing in the COVID-19 pandemic that touched the world. As terrible as the virus is, the economic fallout threatens to be even worse.

Three weeks before this sickness touched the whole world I had what I esteemed to be a prophetic dream. In my dream, I was standing next to the United States president, Donald Trump. I was bouncing up against his shoulder with mine. I was playing with him and joking around. As I continued to do this, he then turned to me and rebuked and chastened me. He said, "This is the presidency of the United States of America." I remember feeling very ashamed and reproved. I realized that I was playing around with something I was supposed to be taking serious. The dream continued. President Trump and I were standing next to each other, with me standing on his left side. There was a table right in front of us. On the table was a newspaper opened to the financial section. President Trump took his hand and began to scan the report on this particular page. He then turned the page of the paper and began to look at the next report. He continued to turn the page time after time until he had looked at the entire financial report. I knew he was investigating and looking at the status of the economy in this report. When he was finished examining the report, he then folded the paper two times and turned and handed it to me. This was the end of the dream.

As I awoke, I was aware of several things as I began to meditate and pray into this dream. One was that something that needed to be taken seriously was not being esteemed on the appropriate level. This is what I was guilty of in my dream. I have been given an assignment to stand with and pray for President Trump since before he was elected. I felt that I had been diligent with this assignment. In my dream however I had become very familiar and playful with what I was to be taking seriously. I do not discount that I need to be more serious and diligent in what God has called me and assigned me to do. However, I believe I represent not just me in the dream, but also the church and intercessors who are to be honoring and esteeming this place we are to be praying for. We are told that we must pray for all that are in authority in I Timothy 2:1-2.

> *Therefore I exhort first of all that supplications, prayers, intercessions, and giving of thanks be made for all men, for kings and all who are in authority, that we may lead a quiet and peaceable life in all godliness and reverence.*

Without proper prayer for those in authority and governmental places, our lives of peace can be disrupted. It is up to the church to take our place in the realms of the spirit, and set things in divine order. Men and women in these places of authority need our prayers that create an atmosphere for them to function in. This allows right decisions to be made by them in these places. We must repent for any lackadaisical and familiar attitude that would cause us to not be serious in the task given us by God.

The other part of the dream is also of great importance. President Trump overseeing the economic status of our nation is critical. I knew when he handed me the paper in the dream that I was being granted an assignment of utmost importance. I knew that our prayers had the power to determine the economic future of nations. As he handed me the paper, I felt there was coming an attack on the economy designed to hinder President Trump's re-election. Remember, this was three weeks before the COVID-19 virus became a worldwide issue and touched the United States. There may be more to the ultimate purpose of this virus, but one of the major issues is too oust President Trump. Those who would espouse globalization and the "one world agenda" detest this man. He is standing in the way of their plans for the world. Also, China has been required under the administration of President Trump to stop taking advantage of the U.S. economically. They would definitely have motives to see the U.S. economy destroyed so President Trump could not be re-elected. They could then see a president put in place in America that would allow them to continue their abuse of the U.S. economically. Trade deficits that other presidents have allowed would be put back into place. There would be a purposeful weakening of the American economy so the One World Order could be propagated and enforced. They know that globalization can never occur as long as there is a strong America. It must be weakened so their deviate plan can prosper.

Regardless of what is driving the reason behind this economic catastrophe, we are watching it happen before our eyes. However, God prophetically showed it beforehand, to let us know we can alter the outcome. Instead of economies being destroyed, we can see them reset. We have been given the assignment to take our place in behalf of the economy of the world. We can stand in the Courts of Heaven and see this dastardly scheme undone, and economies restored. It will take our prayers however. It will take us being serious and recognizing the place we have been given.

In every crisis there is an opportunity. In fact one of the definitions for crisis is "a dangerous opportunity." Right now it would look like we are in danger. Everything could economically collapse. There is even talk of a *depression*. I remember my parents telling of living through the *depression*. They told of being without food, needs going unmet and life being hard. However, this is not the intent of the Lord. This is the reason for the assignment. We must take what has been handed to us and pray that economies will be reset and not destroyed. We must recognize the opportunity that is in this crisis and not allow the danger part to overwhelm us. We need to pray, move in wisdom and exercise our faith in the goodness of our God. We can see not only our own economic status rearranged for good, but also be a part of answering the cry of a culture. We can come through this seeing the merciful hand of God, rather than the cruelties of the devil revealed. Economies can be reset rather than destroyed.

CHAPTER 2

PERSONAL AND CULTURAL DELIVERANCE

When we think of financial troubles, we normally think of it from a personal place. This is because we all have responsibilities, families to take care of and needs to meet. The threat of this being interrupted can be very frightening and scary. God has a solution to this, just like every other thing. However, there is also deliverance from the Lord for cultures as a whole. In other words, not only can God meet our needs,

He can save the economies of nations. We are not just called to see our own problems solved, we are also called to see the troubles of nations healed. When God meets our individual needs, a handful of problems are solved. When He, however, moves in behalf of nations and its cultures, the multitudes see their needs met and problems eradicated. We can see these two spheres depicted in scripture. During the days of Elijah, the widow of Zarephath had her own personal economy healed. There had been a drought and famine in Israel as a result of there being no rain for years. This woman had come to the end of her provision. She is in the process of building a fire to make the last meal for her and her son. In this hopeless situation, she is met by the prophet Elijah. God has sent him to her, to not only save her house in this catastrophic economic time, but also for her to save him. We see this in I Kings 17:10-16. As the woman obeyed the words of the prophet of God, supernatural provision came to her house.

> *So he arose and went to Zarephath. And when he came to the gate of the city, indeed a widow was there gathering sticks. And he called to her and said, "Please bring me a little water in a cup, that I may drink." And as she was going to get it, he called to her and said, "Please bring me a morsel of bread in your hand."*

> *So she said, "As the Lord your God lives, I do not have bread, only a handful of flour in a bin, and a little oil in a jar; and see, I am gathering a couple of sticks that I may go in and prepare it for myself and my son, that we may eat it, and die."*

And Elijah said to her, "Do not fear; go and do as you have said, but make me a small cake from it first, and bring it to me; and afterward make some for yourself and your son. For thus says the Lord God of Israel: 'The bin of flour shall not be used up, nor shall the jar of oil run dry, until the day the Lord sends rain on the earth.'"

So she went away and did according to the word of Elijah; and she and he and her household ate for many days. The bin of flour was not used up, nor did the jar of oil run dry, according to the word of the Lord which He spoke by Elijah.

When this woman moved at the word of the Lord, she stepped from one economic system to another. She moved from the *world's economic system* to *God's economic system*. Paul promised the Philippi church that there was another system they could be engaged in in Philippians 4:16-19:

> *For even in Thessalonica you sent aid once and again for my necessities. Not that I seek the gift, but I seek the fruit that abounds to your account. Indeed I have all and abound. I am full, having received from Epaphroditus the things sent from you, a sweet-smelling aroma, an acceptable sacrifice, well pleasing to God. And my God shall supply all your need according to His riches in glory by Christ Jesus.*

As a result of the Philippians' consistent giving into Paul's life, they were now in another economic place in the unseen world. Paul declared that God would *supply their need according to His riches in glory.* The source of the supply was *His riches in glory.* The source was not the economy of Philippi. This was not what God was limited to when supplying their need. His only limitation was *His riches in glory.* This means there was *no limitations.* These people were now living and operating in a different economic system. They were not constrained by the world's economy. They were now a part of a limitless economy, where there was no need or lack. This is what the widow of Zarephath stepped into. When she put the prophet first, she transitioned to the economy of heaven. Therefore the rules that applied to others no longer applied to her. She was now living and functioning in an economy that knew nothing of lack and need.

We too can move into this economy on a personal level for our families. It will, however, require us to obey the word of the Lord. It will demand that we move in faith and even do the unthinkable. This woman took her last, turned it into her first, through giving it to the prophet who represented God, and received her miracle. She went from having no future, to having a destiny arranged by God because of her raw faith and willingness to obey. Her activity caused her to move into a new economy that allowed constant provision for her, her family and the man of God. This is the way we see God's hand move for us economically on a personal level.

If we are to see a cultural blessing come to the economy of nations, we must apply some other secrets. Jeremiah 29:7 shows the prophet giving a people in captivity some counsel and wisdom.

And seek the peace of the city where I have caused you to be carried away captive, and pray to the Lord for it; for in its peace you will have peace.

The false prophets were telling the people of God that they were not going to be in captivity for a long period. They were convincing them that God was going to deliver them and take them back to their land. However, Jeremiah is telling them this isn't true. He is actually telling them this captivity is going to last 70 years. Therefore, he is admonishing them to lose a temporary mindset and realize this is their new home. He tells them to marry wives, plant gardens, build houses, and plan to be in this situation for several generations. He then tells them to *seek the peace of the city, for in its peace they will have peace.* In other words,

Jeremiah is exhorting the people of God to contend for the well-being of the culture.

There are a couple of significant ideas associated with this. First of all when we talk of peace, it is the word *shalom*. It means "safety, nothing missing, nothing left out, prosperity." When Jeremiah tells them to seek this *peace*, he is encouraging them to work for the economic well-being of the city among other realms of *peace*. He reminds them that in the peace/prosperity of the city, they will have peace and prosperity themselves. Even though we can see God bless us as individuals and families, when the territory we are a part of is blessed, we can be blessed as well. The Lord is reminding His people that their prosperity and increase can be affected by the condition present in the economy of the culture they are a part of. He therefore declares they should contend and war for the blessing to come on this place. It is so for us today. When economies are blessed in a region, territory, city and/or nation it becomes easier to prosper in those settings.

The second idea connected here is *we have the power and authority to determine this economic status*. Jeremiah told them they should *seek the peace* in the situation. This means they could determine what the financial condition was. This is quite amazing, because these were Jews who were captives and foreigners in a strong land. Yet God is saying they have the authority to determine the peace/prosperity that would be within this culture. This is so because of the principle found in I Corinthians 7:14. In this scripture we see Paul explaining that if a spouse believes, they *sanctify* the home even though the other spouse might not be a believer. The believing part *sanctifies* the unbelieving part so the blessing of God might come on it.

> *For the unbelieving husband is sanctified by the wife, and the unbelieving wife is sanctified by the husband; otherwise your children would be unclean, but now they are holy.*

This means that God is able to claim the home as His own because the believing part allows the blessing of God to come. This is what something being considered to be *holy* means. When something is holy it means it belongs to God and He now has the right to bless and prosper it. This is what can happen in a culture that is even god-less. If the believers know how to operate and move in a culture, they can determine what happens in the culture, rather than the unbelieving part. The Lord will honor their presence and move to establish His blessing for the sake of those who belong to Him. They can *seek the peace* and determine what the economic status of the region will be. This was the command of God to Israel in Babylonian captivity. It is His command to us today. We are to function as His people in the culture we are a part of. As we do, that culture's economic condition can be blessed of God. The result will be that not only is the culture prosperous, but we, as a part of it are freed to prosper as well. Let us take our place as those God would use to effect nations and see them prosper and increase.

CHAPTER 3

SECRET #1 – BUILDING A HOUSE OF PRAYER

When we are contending for our own personal breakthrough and blessing economically, we ourselves are sufficient. In other words, we have the right and authority to petition the Lord for ourselves and our families. If however, we are to see a nation and its culture come into economic peace and prosperity, there must be a *house* that can represent it before the Lord and His Courts. This is a hidden secret that I believe we are just now beginning to recognize. Isaiah 56:7 gives us an idea concerning this insight.

> *Even them I will bring to My holy mountain,*
>
> *And make them joyful in My house of prayer.*
>
> *Their burnt offerings and their sacrifices*
>
> *Will be accepted on My altar;*
>
> *For My house shall be called a house of prayer for all nations.*

When I speak of a house, I am speaking of that which is corporate, with multiples of people being built together. This is what a house implies. In other words, it is a people, perhaps from diverse backgrounds that are mixed and joined together for a common purpose and intent. Relationships are formed from a perspective of commitment and covenant that allows us to be considered a house before God. This is very important. Notice that God's *house* will be a *"house of prayer **for** all nations."* This means that a house of prayer is that which can represent nations before the Lord. In other words, the house is granted the right to operate as a government to represent a culture before the Lord. This is what our governments do. They are people who are normally elected and stand in a place to represent the people who elected them. As they function, their activity produces decisions that determine life among those they represent. This is what a house of prayer does before the Lord. It stands as that which God accepts in behalf of the culture it is a part of. This is why every culture/nations needs a house of prayer functioning in its behalf. It is not enough that individual people are praying.

The ways of God demand that there be a house to stand in behalf of a culture. This is what allows God to respond to a nation. The whole nation/culture doesn't have to repent or cry out to God. If there is a house of prayer for that culture then God accepts it just as if the whole nation is calling to Him. This is what God was looking for in Sodom and Gomorrah as a result of Abraham standing before Him. In finality to Abraham's contending for mercy for Sodom and Gomorrah, God agreed to spare it if there were ten righteous. We read in Genesis 18:32:

> *Then he said, "Let not the Lord be angry, and I will speak but once more: Suppose ten should be found there?"*
>
> *And He said, "I will not destroy it for the sake of ten."*

When the Lord agreed for ten righteous to represent Sodom and Gomorrah before Him, He was agreeing to the influence of a house of prayer. I had wondered why Abraham couldn't simply request mercy of the Lord for Sodom and Gomorrah. I then realized that Abraham wasn't a part of that culture. The principle is that only a prayer house from within a culture can represent that culture before the Lord. This is what God was looking for. The sad fact was there wasn't a house of prayer in Sodom and Gomorrah that could stand in its behalf. The result was Sodom and Gomorrah was destroyed. The absence of a house of prayer in behalf of a culture will cause it to forfeit any and all mercy the Lord would desire to show to it.

We must have not just individuals who cry to God for a culture, but a house. There must be a corporate people who heaven can receive as a house to represent nations and their culture before the Lord. Without this, we will not see the goodness of the Lord manifested. Nations will be destroyed, cultures will be attacked and people's lives will be upended. If however there is a house that has been built and recognized before the Lord, we will be able to appeal to the Lord and see His kindness and mercy revealed. Breakthroughs will come because God who is Judge of all is able to hear the case presented by this house and show mercy to the culture it represents. The lack of a house of prayer, in my opinion, is the reason behind any lack of results we have seen in our prayers. The lack of results is not a result of effort, or even genuine faith or godly desire. The lack of results is because we haven't had a house that heaven could recognize.

A house is that which has been built together in some form of covenant relationships. It is not a prayer network or a big ministry or even a well-oiled organization. A house is a family that is formed through covenant. All the other things I just mentioned are built easily enough. There is nothing wrong with any of them. However, a family and its operation is something completely different. If there is conflict in the aforementioned things, then people are just fired, leave or are dismissed. Life moves on. In family however, there is a need and mandate to resolve the conflict. Covenant demands this. I have often said that covenant takes the back door out of relationships. In other words, when you are in covenant with someone you can't just leave or run away. You must by virtue of the covenant stand and deal with the conflict and see peace and resolution come. This is what happens in a house.

Mary and I have six children; five of them are married and we have seven grandchildren. When there is conflict in our house/ family we don't cease to be a family. We are pressed to sit and deal with the problem until it is solved. This is what godly families do. What I have described is one of the main reasons why our prayers have not been answered. It is because instead of dealing with conflict, we run. This gives the devil the legal right to question that we are a true house. A true house abides by covenant measure. If however, we take the easy way out instead of solving our problems, this gives room to the accuser, the devil to make a case against us. He uses this to deny us the right as a house to present a case for God as Judge to render a decision in our behalf. We must repent for not operating as a house. When we do and we begin to stand as a true house of prayer, we will be able to present cases that will get results. We will represent cultures before the Lord and see Him as Judge render decisions that allow His passion to be fulfilled and Satan's strategies revoked. May we be His house of prayer!

CHAPTER 4

SECRET #2 – PRESENTING PROPHETIC WORDS

Once we are operating as a house of prayer to represent a culture, we can then approach the Courts of Heaven. As we by faith come near His Courts, we are there to present cases before Him in behalf of the culture we represent. One of the main ways we do this is by presenting prophetic destiny and words from God that have been revealed. We see this in Daniel 7:9-10.

I watched till thrones were put in place,

And the Ancient of Days was seated;

His garment was white as snow,

And the hair of His head was like pure wool.

His throne was a fiery flame,

Its wheels a burning fire;

A fiery stream issued

And came forth from before Him.

A thousand thousands ministered to Him;

Ten thousand times ten thousand stood before Him.

The court was seated,

And the books were opened.

Notice that the Court is seated and the books are open. Books that are in heaven contain prophetic destinies. We see this is

Psalm 139:16 where David speaks of books that concern him.

> *Your eyes saw my substance, being yet unformed.*
>
> *And in Your book they all were written,*
>
> *The days fashioned for me,*
>
> *When as yet there were none of them.*

Two things are specifically contained in this book that David spoke of. Our substance yet unformed is in these books. I take this to be my DNA that determines my interest, my likes, my abilities and the things I gravitate toward. This was all set in place concerning me before time began. This is what II Timothy 1:9 actually communicates.

Who has saved us and called us with a holy calling, not according to our works, but according to His own purpose and grace which was given to us in Christ Jesus before time began.

Notice that *purpose and grace* were given to us before time began. This means that before anything existed God had already determined the purpose for my existence. He had also given me grace for that purpose. The grace that has already been apportioned to me determines my interest, my likes, my abilities and that which I gravitate toward. It is designed this way so I may fulfill the purpose for which I exist and was created. This is what is in the book in heaven concerning me. The other thing that is in my book is *my days yet unfashioned*. This is referring to how long I will live and what I am supposed to do. Paul actually spoke of this in Ephesians 2:10. He talks of the works that were planned beforehand for us.

> *For we are His workmanship, created in Christ Jesus for good works, which God prepared beforehand that we should walk in them.*

The Lord ordained what we were to accomplish in His purposes. Everything that would cause us to gravitate toward this and have the ability to do it was prepared beforehand. This means it was written in His book, foreordained and predestined. This doesn't mean we are His puppet. We have a free will and can choose a way other than what He has ordained. This will almost always lead to sorrow and sadness. It will at least lead to a sense of dissatisfaction and lack of fulfillment. If however, we discern and agree with what is in the books of heaven concerning us, we will find the joy of life that has been reserved for us. Purpose and destiny are not something we create. They are that which we discover has already been arranged for us by our loving God.

Once we discern prophetically what God has planned for us, we then take that and present it before the Courts of Heaven. This is why the Court was seated and the books were opened. The *opened* books allow us to see into and realize what we were made for. Holy desires and longings fill our hearts. From these desires, we begin to ask the Lord for what He has arranged for us. This is us presenting what is the prophetic purpose of God concerning us in His Courts. This is very similar to a lawyer standing in a natural court and presenting testimony before a judge. Once the testimony is presented the judge can then render a decision. Judges can only render decisions based on the testimony presented. This is true of God as Judge as well. When we come before the Courts of Heaven and petition the Lord based on what He wrote about us in His books, this is very powerful. It gives the Lord the right to answer the cry of our heart, fulfill our godly desires, and God gets His will done in the earth. We do this as individuals, but also as a corporate people called a house of prayer. When we come before the Lord as a house of prayer, we are presenting His prophetic desire for nations. We are petitioning Him that His will would be done and any interruption of it by the devil would be judged as illegal and unrighteous. This can all be the result of us, as a house of prayer, asking for the

Lord to render judgments in behalf of us and His purposes and desires.

As we discern His prophetic desire over nations through intercession, prophetic words, unctions of the Holy Spirit and visitations from God, we can bring this into the Courts of Heaven. We can request that the passion of God revealed through prophetic insight out of the books of heaven be fulfilled. Once we understand this, we can tread the Courts of Heaven as those commissioned of God to be there. We can cry to the Lord of heaven and request that His longing be fulfilled. There is no greater or noble purpose in earth than God allowing us to be a part of the process of heaven coming to earth. As we cry from this prophetic unction and present cases in the Courts of Heaven, decisions are rendered and God's will is done. What a glorious process we have been allowed to be a part of. Let us arise and petition His Courts. We will see His kingdom come and His will be done on earth even as it is in heaven!

CHAPTER 5

SECRET #3 – UNDOING WORDS OF JUDGMENT

As we contend for the resetting of economies, there are things that we must undo that would seek to hinder this. Many times we, as the people of God, are those who unwittingly empower the intent of the devil rather than the purposes of God. This can be done by those who are prophesying judgment rather than recovery and restoration. As we entered the time of contending against this virus called COVID 19, I was leading a session with a group of international intercessors and apostolic leaders online. We were petitioning the Courts of Heaven for the power of the virus to be broken, but also for economies to be reset. As we were petitioning the Courts, interceding and crying to the Lord, I became aware of words of judgment that were speaking before the Courts and being used to do just the opposite of what we were requesting. I knew that I needed to undo these words of judgment so that they might not empower the intent of the devil against us. The devil would like to destroy economies. God's passion is to reset them. However, there were and are people of God who are proclaiming this to be the judgment of God rather than the works of Satan. We might think that people erroneously declaring judgment rather than mercy would have no effect. This is not true. Whatever prophetic report we bring becomes testimony before the Courts of Heaven. Even if it is not in agreement with God's word, the devil will take this report and use it as evidence for his plan to be done. He actually takes the word and voice of God's people and uses it to petition the Lord for the judgment they are pronouncing. Even if this isn't the Lord's desire, the Court will hear the devil's case. The Lord told me, I needed to undo these words of these supposed prophets that they might not stand and speak in the Courts of Heaven. Let me explain this from the Word of God.

When Israel came to the border of the Promised Land, Moses sent twelve spies across to look at the land. They were in the land for 40 days. They then came back with their report based on their investigation. Ten spies said it was a good land

and everything, plus more, of what they had heard, dreamed and believed it to be. However, there were giants, walled cities and iron chariots there. They were not able to take the land. If they tried, they would be defeated and destroyed as a people. They and their little ones would perish. We find this report in Numbers 13:31-33.

> *But the men who had gone up with him said, "We are not able to go up against the people, for they are stronger than we." And they gave the children of Israel a bad report of the land which they had spied out, saying, "The land through which we have gone as spies is a land that devours its inhabitants, and all the people whom we saw in it are men of great stature. There we saw the giants (the descendants of Anak came from the giants); and we were like grasshoppers*

in our own sight, and so we were in their sight."

They were convinced that God was not big enough and powerful enough to deliver the nations into their hands. They caused the heart of the people to melt. The problem was this report wasn't just heard by the people, it was heard in the Courts of Heaven. This report became prophetic testimony. Based on the testimony of these ten spies God rendered a judgment and a decision. Numbers 14:34 shows God as Judge basing His decision on the report of these ten spies/leaders of Israel.

According to the number of the days in which you spied out the land, forty days, for each day you shall bear your guilt one year, namely forty years, and you shall know My rejection.

God sentenced them to 40 years of wandering in the wilderness. The sentence was based on a year for each day the spies were in the land. Even though there were two spies, Joshua and Caleb, who brought a good report, the words of the ten spoke great volume in the Courts of Heaven. The testimony of the ten before the Courts of Heaven determined the destiny of a nation for the next 40 years. It wasn't in agreement with God's original design or intent. Yet their testimony before His Courts caused the God of all the earth to render a decision. A judge can only render verdicts based on evidence given. When these ten gave their report/testimony, the devil used it to speak against a nation.

We must be careful of our report. We also must come before the Lord and silence any word that would be not in agreement with His prophetic destiny. Words of doubt, unbelief, judgment and condemnation have power when spoken in the Courts of Heaven. We cannot afford to have these words not dealt with in His Courts. We, as His people, who understand His heart, must approach the Court, repent for the words spoken and ask for them to be annulled by the Blood of Jesus. We can request that they will not be allowed as evidence into the Court proceeding concerning the economy of nations. We have a right as a house of prayer to request this and ask for these words and their effect to be revoked. As we do this, we can present in their place the prophetic intent of the Lord and His gracious character. As we do, that which would speak against us, the economies of the earth, and God's passion, will be removed and silenced. The result will be economies reset and not destroyed. What

God desires will be realized and not the torment and cruelty of the devil!

CHAPTER 6

SECRET #4 – GOD'S LOVE FOR PEOPLE

In dealing with the crisis of COVID 19 and its destructive effect against economies, we must have the wisdom of the Lord in how to present cases in the Courts of Heaven. We are told that the Holy Spirit is the *parakletos*. This is the Greek word for *Helper* as revealed in John 14:16.

And I will pray the Father, and He will give you another Helper, that He may abide with you forever.

Parakletos means "an intercessor, advocate, a legal aid." As we approach the Courts of Heaven it is the Holy Spirit that helps us know how to present an effective case in these Courts. He is our legal aid. This is why Romans 8:26 tells us that He helps us when we don't know how to pray, or even what to pray.

Likewise the Spirit also helps in our weaknesses. For we do not know what we should pray for as we ought, but the Spirit Himself makes intercession for us with groanings which cannot be uttered.

58

Only through the power of the Holy Spirit and His influence, can we effectively function in the Courts of Heaven. He will show us how and what we are to present. It is not enough to just understand principles when functioning in the Courts of Heaven. We cannot turn the process into a formula. This will not bring us the results we desire and even what God wants. We must move under the direction and unction of the Holy Spirit. He will cause us to know how to petition the Courts effectively.

In dealing with the economic fall-out of COVID 19, the Lord gave me a means of approaching the Courts of Heaven effectively. In the midst of everything else we have done, the Lord told me to *remind* Him of His love for people. First of all, why would I *need* to remind God of His love? Remember that we are presenting a case. God knows He loves people, however in a Court setting this needs to be presented as evidence. This is what gives the Lord as Judge the right to move and answer our request. Even though God is aware of things, He *needs* us to remind Him as Judge. This is what Isaiah 43:26 tells us.

Put Me in remembrance;

Let us contend together;

State your case, that you may be acquitted.

When we remind the Lord and *put Him in remembrance*, we are stating our case. We are causing the Lord as Judge to hear the petition and be granted testimony that would allow the verdict we are seeking. When the Lord told me to *remind* Him of His love for people, I knew it was connected to what David did in I Chronicles 21:17. David had sinned by numbering

Israel. There are several things connected to this, but it was out of a fleshly heart that David had done this. Most likely, it was about David boasting in the flesh of how powerful he was a king and not having his confidence in God. Regardless, his activity offended God. As a result, a plague had broken out among the people and thousands were perishing. As David witnesses this, he is moved to cry out to the Lord.

> *And David said to God, "Was it not I who commanded the people to be numbered? I am the one who has sinned and done evil indeed; but these sheep, what have they done? Let Your hand, I pray, O Lord my God, be against me and my father's house, but not against Your people that they should be plagued."*

61

As David seeks to stop the plague, he takes ownership of what he has done. He admits it is his fault. He then petitions the Lord and cries out for the people. He ask God to let him and his house suffer but not the people. He is asking the Lord to spare the people out of God's care and love for them. The Lord actually then allows David to bring an offering that would speak in behalf of him, his house, and the people. The plague is stopped as a result. However, it was David's cry for mercy toward the people out of God's love for them that produced this. We must realize that God loves people. We can use this to petition His Courts concerning the economic fallout of COVID 19. We can cause God to remember the devastation, suffering, and harm economies destroyed would bring. We can call the Lord into remembrance and ask that there would be mercy from His Court rendered.

The result would be the resetting of economies and not the destruction of them.

This is what happened when God relented of destroying Nineveh in the days of Jonah. Jonah was an angry prophet who wanted Nineveh destroyed. After he had proclaimed judgment and its destruction, he positioned himself to see what would happen. The problem for Jonah was Nineveh repented, from the king all the way down to the common people. Therefore, God desired to show mercy. This caused Jonah great anger. God left off dealing with Nineveh and dealt with His prophet. The Lord allowed a plant to grown to shade Jonah from the elements. He then destroyed the plant and brought Jonah to a realization. In Jonah 4:10-11 we see God's discourse with His disgruntled prophet. We, however, see God's reasoning for showing mercy to Nineveh and not judging it.

> *But the Lord said, "You have had pity on the plant for which you have not labored, nor made it grow, which came up in a night and perished in a night. And should I not pity Nineveh, that great city, in which are more than one hundred and twenty thousand persons who cannot discern between their right hand and their left—and much livestock?"*

God tells Jonah that just like he had pity on a plant he didn't produce, God would have pity on a people where many folks were present. He said to Jonah, *"should I not pity these 120,000 people who know nothing of Me? And also should I not spare the animals and livestock?"* Notice God's care and love for people, animals and His creation. God's reasoning for sparing Nineveh was He cared! We have a right to petition the Lord on the basis of His love, His care, and His concern. We can approach His Courts and ask that because He cares for people, economies would be reset. We can remind Him of how difficult it would be for the multitudes and ask that mercy would be shown. Our God is a loving, kind, and gratuitous God. He will hear our cry and answer. Approach His Courts because of His great love and concern over people.

CHAPTER 7

SECRET #5 – OFFERINGS THAT SPEAK

The final secret that can move God as Judge is to offer offering in His Courts. There are those who will have a difficulty with this. They, however, do not realize the place that our offerings have before the Lord. Offerings have voice that speaks in the Courts of Heaven in behalf of those who bring them. This is clearly seen in Cornelius' experience in Acts 10:3-4. An angel appears to Cornelius and instructs him. He also tells him why he has come.

> *About the ninth hour of the day he saw clearly in a vision an angel of God coming in and saying to him, "Cornelius!"*

> *And when he observed him, he was afraid, and said, "What is it, lord?"*

> *So he said to him, "Your prayers and your alms have come up for a memorial before God."*

The angel says he has been sent to him because his prayers and his giving have created a memorial before God. A memorial simply means that something is speaking that is causing God to remember. Cornelius' praying and giving have released a sound, a voice and a influence that has grabbed God's attention. The result is this angel has been sent. When everything is said and done, God uses the house of Cornelius as a gate through which the Holy Spirit enters the Gentile world. What caused God to choose Cornelius' house above all the houses? It is very simple. He had something speaking that caused God to remember him. This memorial was created by his prayers and giving. We see this also in Numbers 10:10 when Moses has the two silver trumpets made. These trumpets were used for a variety of things. They, however, were to be used to blow over offerings. Trumpets speak of prophetic prayer and releases. They are declarations and announcements. This is a part of what praying is. Notice that as these trumpets sound over offerings, memorials are created.

Also in the day of your gladness, in your appointed feasts, and at the beginning of your months, you shall blow the trumpets over your burnt offerings and over the sacrifices of your peace offerings; and they shall be a memorial for you before your God: I am the Lord your God.

Again we see that when prayers and prophetic releases are mixed with giving, memorials are fashioned. Something begins to speak before God that causes Him to remember us. This is essential to bringing cases before the Courts of Heaven. Remember, *putting Him in remembrance is presenting cases in the Courts* (see Isaiah 43:26). When I bring my petition and mix offerings with it, it can create that which causes God to remember me. This is why as a house of prayer we see God accepting offerings as in Isaiah 56:7.

> *Even them I will bring to My holy mountain,*
>
> *And make them joyful in My house of prayer.*
>
> *Their burnt offerings and their sacrifices*
>
> *Will be accepted on My altar;*
>
> *For My house shall be called a house of prayer for all nations.*

Part of the function of a house of prayer representing cultures and nations before the Lord is to bring offerings as well. This creates memorials that speak before God and allows decisions to be rendered in behalf of those cultures. As we function as individuals and also houses of prayer, we must mix offerings with our prayers. These offerings will speak and cause the Judge of all the earth to remember us. This is what Noah did in Genesis 8:20-22 as the first business after he came out of the ark. He built an altar and brought an offering to the Lord.

Then Noah built an altar to the Lord, and took of every clean animal and of every clean bird, and offered burnt offerings on the altar. And the Lord smelled a soothing aroma. Then the Lord said in His heart, "I will never again curse the ground for man's sake, although the imagination of man's heart is evil from his youth; nor will I again destroy every living thing as I have done. While the earth remains, seedtime and harvest, cold and heat, winter and summer, and day and night shall not cease."

The result of Noah building an altar and bringing an offering was God making judicial decrees. He made two. The first one was *no more curse*! As we mix offerings with our prayers, it can grant God as Judge the legal right to revoke every curse against us. COVID 19 is a curse. May the Lord remember us because of our prayers and offering and judge COVID 19 as an illegal and unrighteous thing. The second this God did as Judge was reset the economy. He declared *seedtime and harvest*. This is economies beginning to function again. From Noah's offering, worship, and prayers, God reset the economies after a worldwide catastrophe. So He can and will do it again. He also reset climates. *Winter and summer, cold and heat, day and night* were reinstated. Anyone who functions in business knows working with *climates* and discerning trends is essential to success and prosperity. God reinstated these as well. From Noah's offering, God remembered. The result was curses revoked and economies reset. May we move in agreement with the Lord, present our cases and see the economies of nations reset. We will also see our own individual economies set into divine order as we apply these principles over our lives and families. Let us petition the God of all, who waits to hear our cry in His Courts!

ABOUT THE AUTHOR

Robert Henderson is a global apostolic leader who operates in revelation and impartation. His teaching empowers the body of Christ to see the hidden truths of Scripture clearly and apply them for breakthrough results. Driven by a mandate to disciple nations through writing and speaking, Robert travels extensively around the globe, teaching on the apostolic, the Kingdom of God, the "Seven Mountains" and most notably, the Courts of Heaven. He has been married to Mary for 40 years. They have six children and five grandchildren. Together they are enjoying life in beautiful Waco, TX.

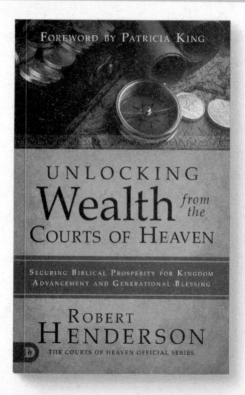

FOREWORD BY PATRICIA KING

UNLOCKING
Wealth *from the*
COURTS OF HEAVEN

SECURING BIBLICAL PROSPERITY FOR KINGDOM
ADVANCEMENT AND GENERATIONAL BLESSING

ROBERT
HENDERSON

THE COURTS OF HEAVEN OFFICIAL SERIES